DISCOVER
The North and the South

by Margaret McNamara

Table of Contents

Introduction	2
Chapter 1 What Was the South Like?	4
Chapter 2 What Was the North Like?	8
Chapter 3 What Was the Civil War Like?	12
Conclusion	18
Concept Map	20
Glossary	22
Index	24

Introduction

Learn about **the North**. Learn about **the South**. Learn about **the Civil War**.

▲ This place was in the South.

▲ This place was in the North.

Words to Know

 factories

 plantations

 slaves

 the Civil War

 the North

 the South

See the Glossary on page 22.

Chapter 1

What Was the South Like?

The South had states.

The South in 1860

▲ These states were in the South.

The South had **plantations**.

▲ This plantation was in the South.

Chapter 1

The South had cotton.

▲ cotton

▲ Cotton fields were in the South.

What Was the South Like?

The South had **slaves**.

It's a Fact
Other people owned the slaves.

▲ Slaves were in the South.

Chapter 2

What Was the North Like?

The North had states.

▲ These states were in the North.

The North had **factories**.

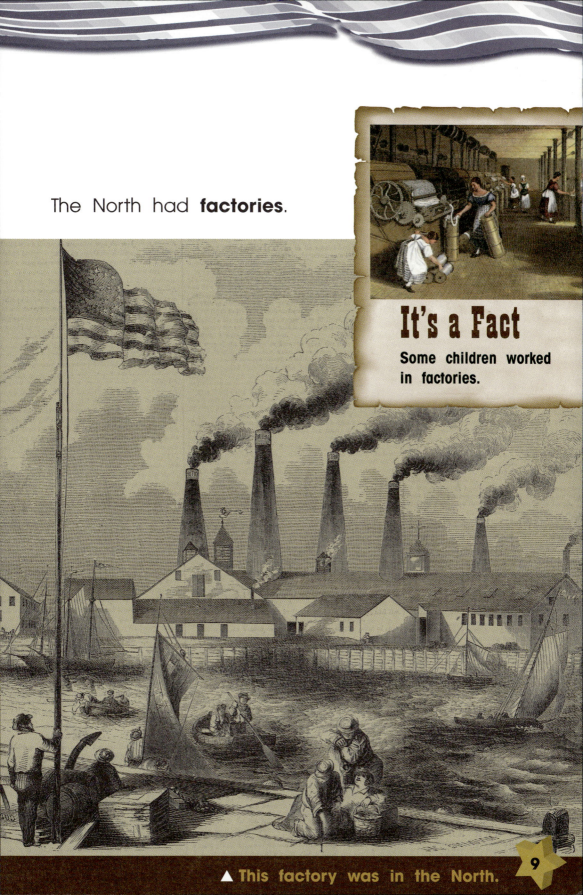

It's a Fact
Some children worked in factories.

▲ This factory was in the North.

Chapter 2

The North had cities.

▲ This city was in the North.

What Was the North Like?

The North had many people.

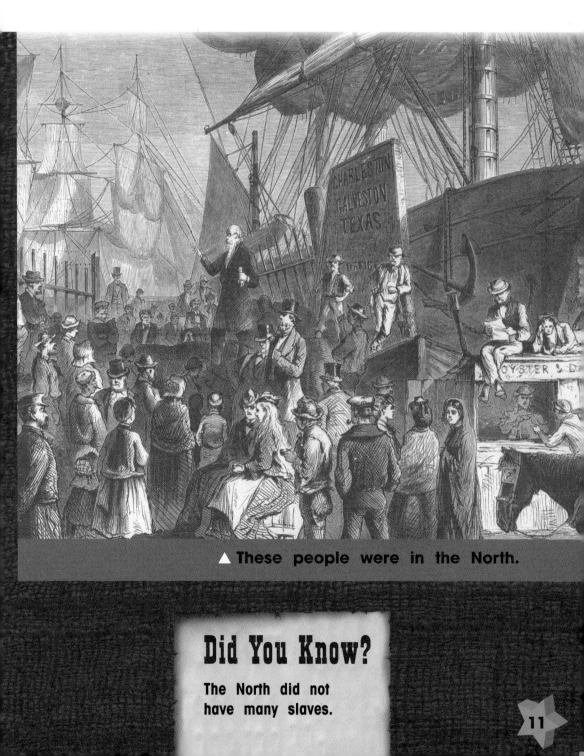

▲ These people were in the North.

Did You Know?
The North did not have many slaves.

Chapter 3

What Was the Civil War Like?

States were in the Civil War.

▲ Northern states were in the Civil War.
Southern states were in the Civil War.

It's a Fact

The Civil War started in 1861.
The Civil War ended in 1865.

States in the Civil War

▲ These states were in the Civil War.

Chapter 3

Soldiers were in the Civil War.

▲ This soldier was from the North.

What Was the Civil War Like?

▲ This soldier was from the South.

Chapter 3

Many battles were in the Civil War.

What Was the Civil War Like?

Big battles were in the Civil War.

It's a Fact
The North won the Civil War.

▲ This battle was in the Civil War.

Conclusion

The North was many states. The South was many states. The Civil War was between the North and the South.

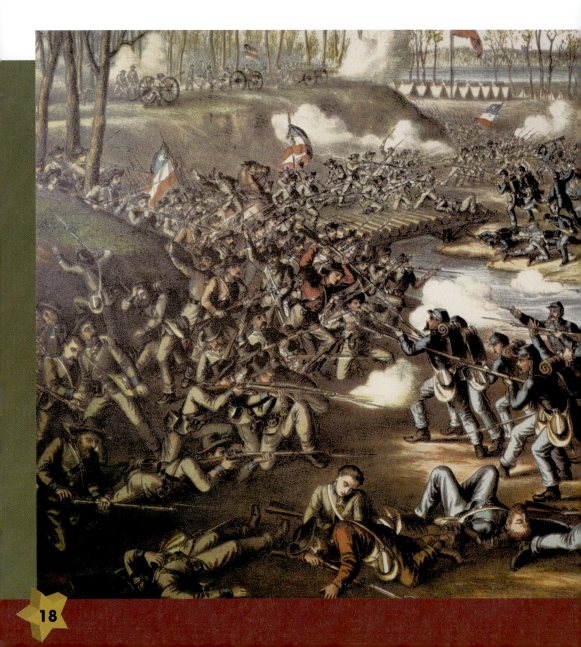

▲ This battle was in the Civil War.

Concept Map

The North and the South

What Was the South Like?
- had states
- had plantations
- had cotton
- had slaves

What Was the North Like?
- had states
- had factories
- had cities
- had many people

What Was the Civil War Like?

- had states
- had soldiers
- had many battles

Glossary

factories buildings where people make things

*The North had **factories**.*

plantations big farms

*The South had **plantations**.*

slaves people owned by other people

*The South had **slaves**.*

the Civil War a war between the states

*States were in **the Civil War**.*

the North the Northern states **the South** the Southern states

The North had states. *The South* had states.

Index

battles, 16–17
cities, 10
Civil War, the, 2, 12, 14, 16–18
cotton, 6
factories, 9
North, the, 2, 8–11, 18
people, 11
plantations, 5
slaves, 7
soldiers, 14
South, the, 2, 4–7, 18
states, 4, 8, 12, 18